Tiny Tinkles Little Musicians Series

BOOK 5

Little Performers PLAY

C D E

Created by **Debra Krol**   Pictures by **Corinne Orazietti & Melanie Hawkins**

This book is dedicated to
all the little people for inspiring me,
and all the BIG people for believing in me.

ISBN (Paperback Perfect Bound): 978-1-990563-04-1

First Edition 2022

TIPS TO HELP YOU TEACH USING THIS BOOK

Welcome to the **Tiny Tinkles Little Musicians Series!** This 5th book in the Little Performers Collection will teach your little musician beginning notation for the notes C, D, and E in both the treble clef and the bass clef. Use the activity cards that are included to help your child become familiar with the location of the notes before beginning the songs. With a little practice, your child will be able to identify all three notes, play lots of games and create moments to explore the keys. Take time to listen and sing the animal sounds, character names and note names! Remember these key words: EXPLORE, LISTEN & PLAY....and your little musician will be set up for successful learning!

I recommend you introduce CDE with fingers 234, but this book gives you the flexibility to introduce with fingers 123 if you prefer. After your little one learns with finger 234, you can restart the book and re-learn the songs with fingers 123.

When your child finishes the book and is comfortable playing CDE, try playing on the group of 3 black keys. Then, try transposing (playing the same finger numbers with different groups of white notes) to different positions on the piano! ABC, GAB, are great to start! These other techniques will help you teach your little musician too:

Keep a STEADY BEAT while you play the patterns and songs in this book.

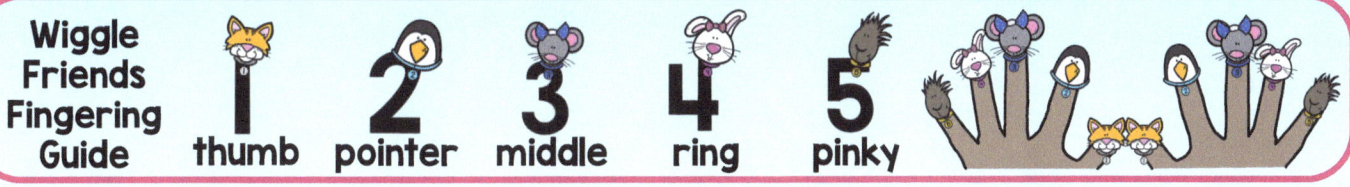

Wiggle Friends Fingering Guide — 1 thumb, 2 pointer, 3 middle, 4 ring, 5 pinky

SING while you play the notes! Your little musician will FEEL the beat and rythm of the music.

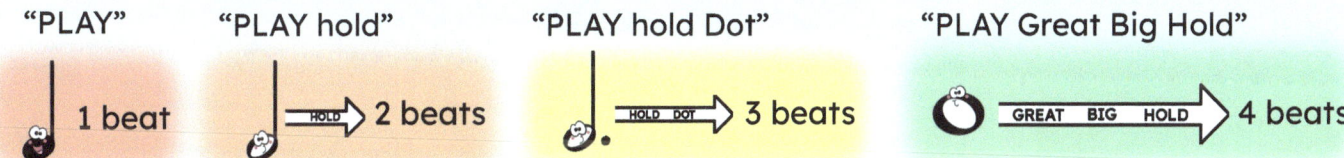

"PLAY" — 1 beat
"PLAY hold" — HOLD 2 beats
"PLAY hold Dot" — HOLD DOT 3 beats
"PLAY Great Big Hold" — GREAT BIG HOLD 4 beats

TIPS TO HELP YOU PRACTICE AND LEARN TOGETHER

- Ask questions like "is it a line or space"
- Count slowly before you begin
- Clap and count the beat before you begin
- Tap the notes and sing LEFT and RIGHT
- Circle patterns or common fingers
- Practice drawing the staff lines and notes
- Play and sing LEFT/RIGHT while you play
- Play and sing or the WORDS while you play
- Try playing all the melodies hands together
- Try transposing to different hand positions

For videos, worksheets, teaching tips and more... please visit: www.tinytinkles.com

Today is a very special day in **Tiny Tinkles Town.**

4

Twoozie is showing **Bobby Bass** and **Tina Treble** how to play his favorite **white keys!**

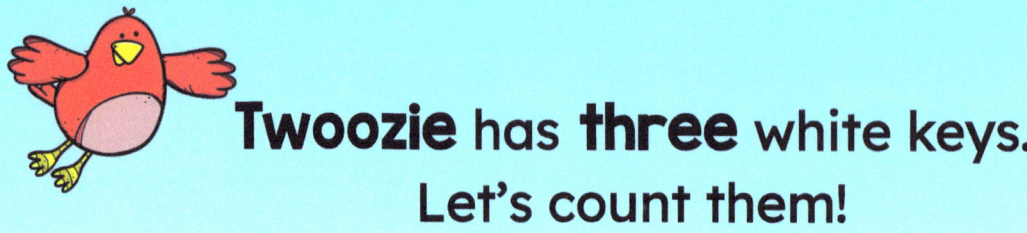

Twoozie has **three** white keys.
Let's count them!

1 2 3

They are the notes **C, D,** and **E.**

Twoozie LOVEs playing **C, D, and E!**

He plays them **down low...**

And he plays them **up high!**

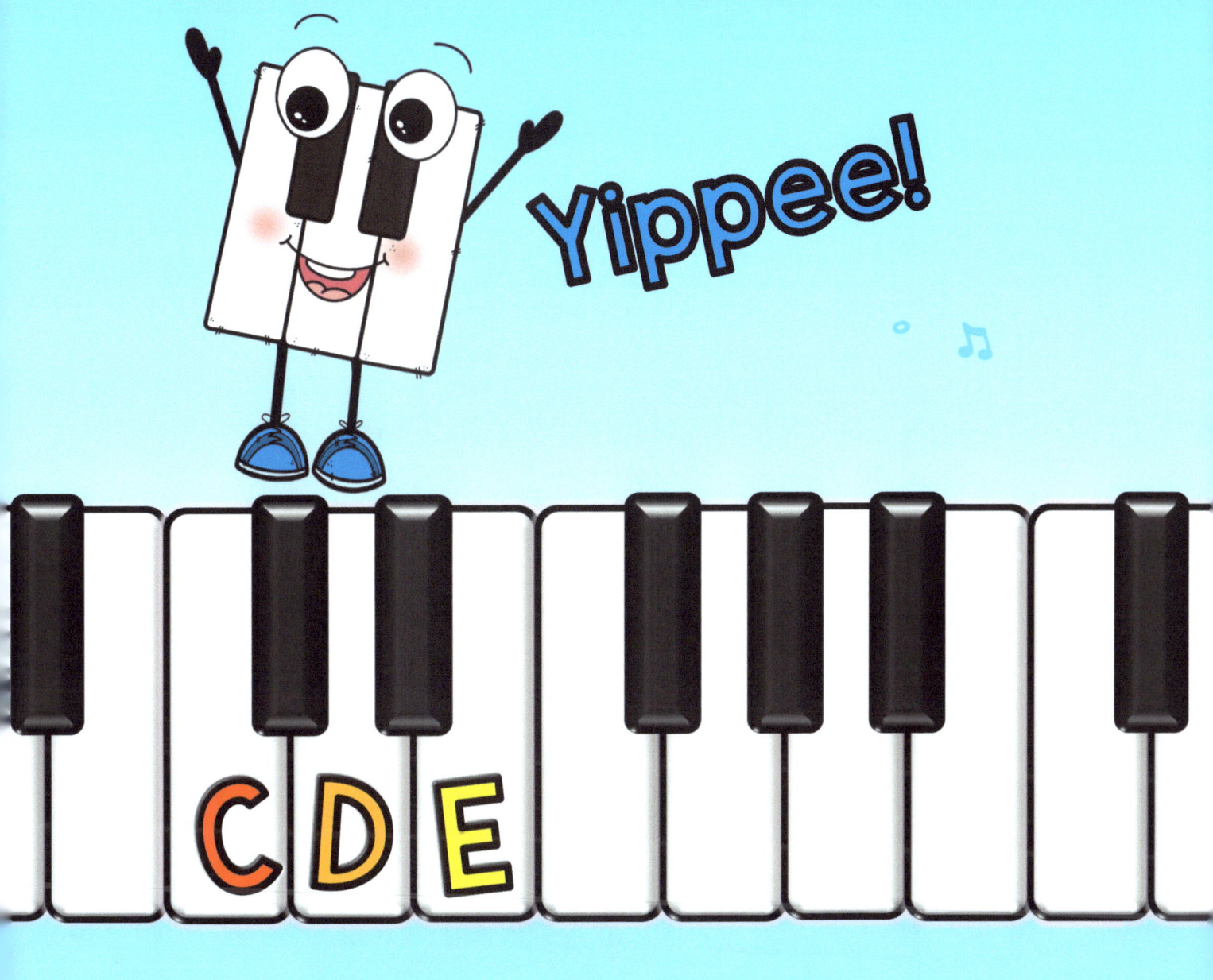

Then, **TWOOZIE** leaps off the piano keys and finds **Middle C, D, and E** in Grammy's Treble Clef!

Zoom!

Tina Treble sings and plays three beautiful **C's** with her **right hand.**

la la la

Then, Tina Treble moves up to the next white keys

and plays three beautiful **D's,** and three amazing **E's!**

Low notes are **Bobby Bass**'s favorite, so he plays a groovy low **C, D,** and **E** in **Grampy's Bass Clef.**

Playing piano is so much fun! **Bobby Bass** moves to the next white keys and plays four **D's** and four **E's!**

Parker Penguin, Missy Mouse and Rosie Rabbit get ready to **wiggle and jiggle!**

"Let's Play SONGS on C, D, and E!"

21

GAMES

1. MATCH - Match the notation cards with the correct piano key.

2. SORT - Sort the cards into categories: Treble Clef notes and Bass Clef notes, C's, D's, or E's, sort into the same rhythmic patterns.

3. PLAY I have, Who has? or Go Fish.

4. PLAY the notes on the cards - shuffle cards, place a few on the fallboard, and practice playing the patterns you see! Start with all the same note, then add new notes as you become more comfortable reading them.

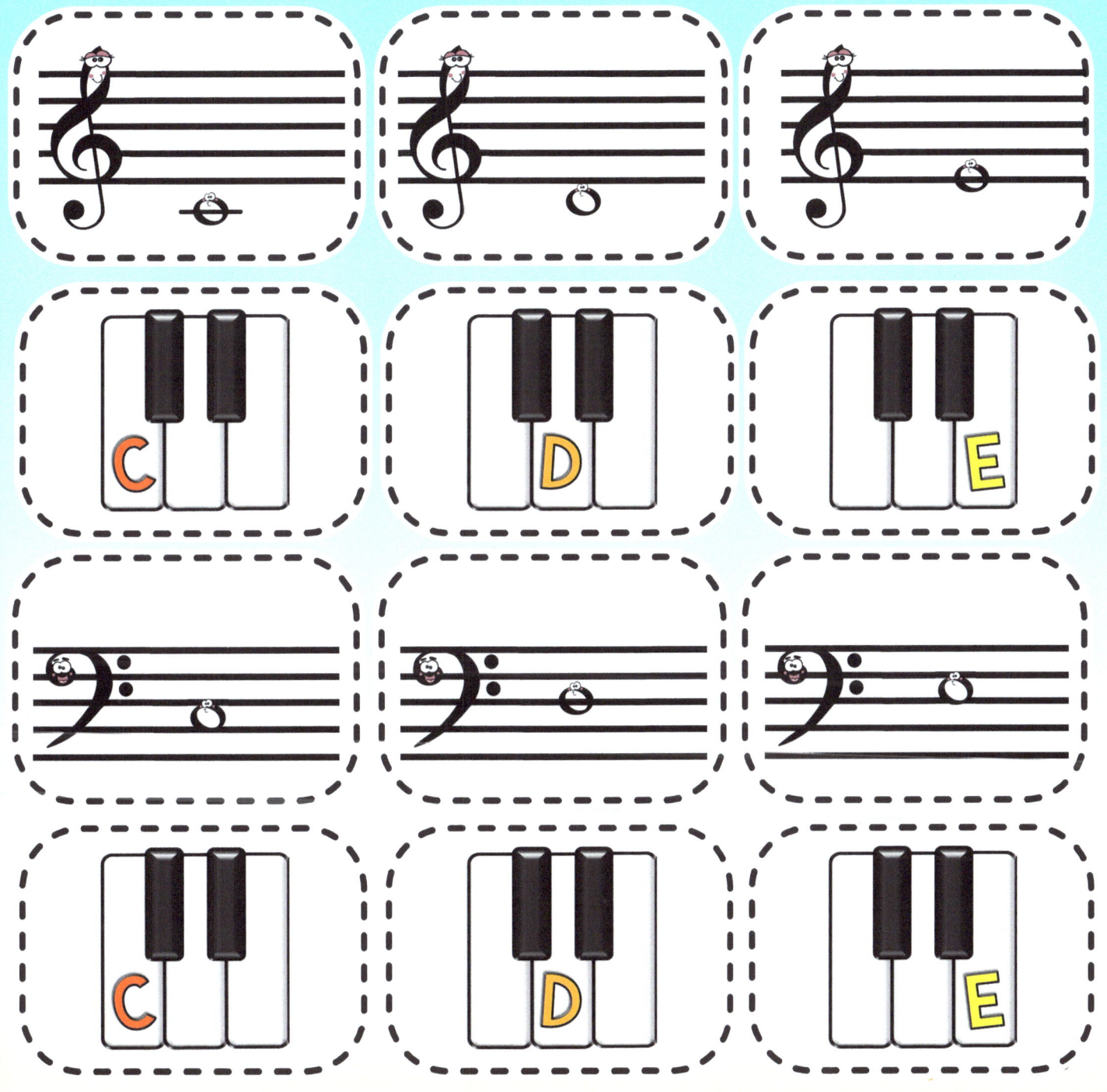

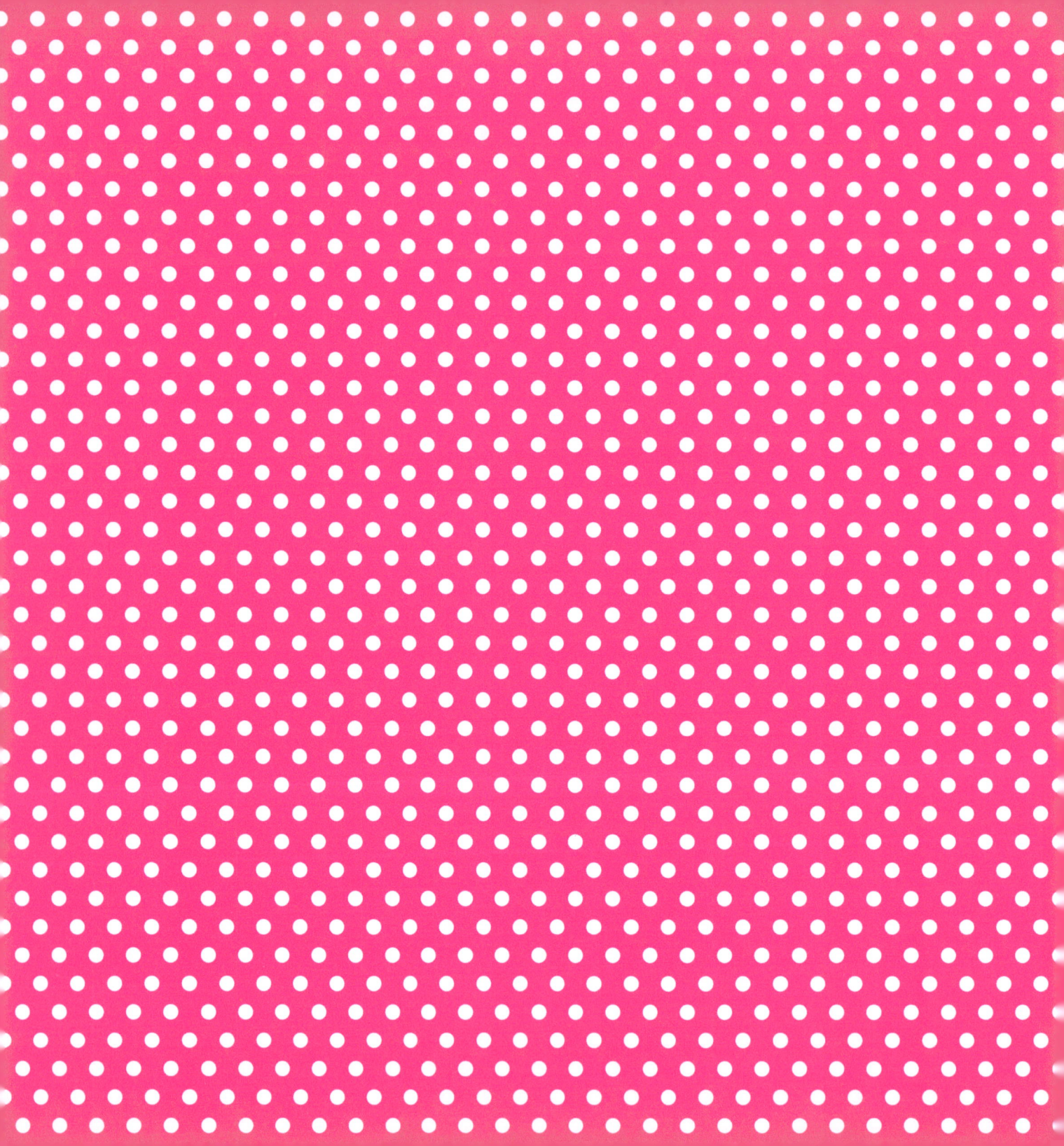

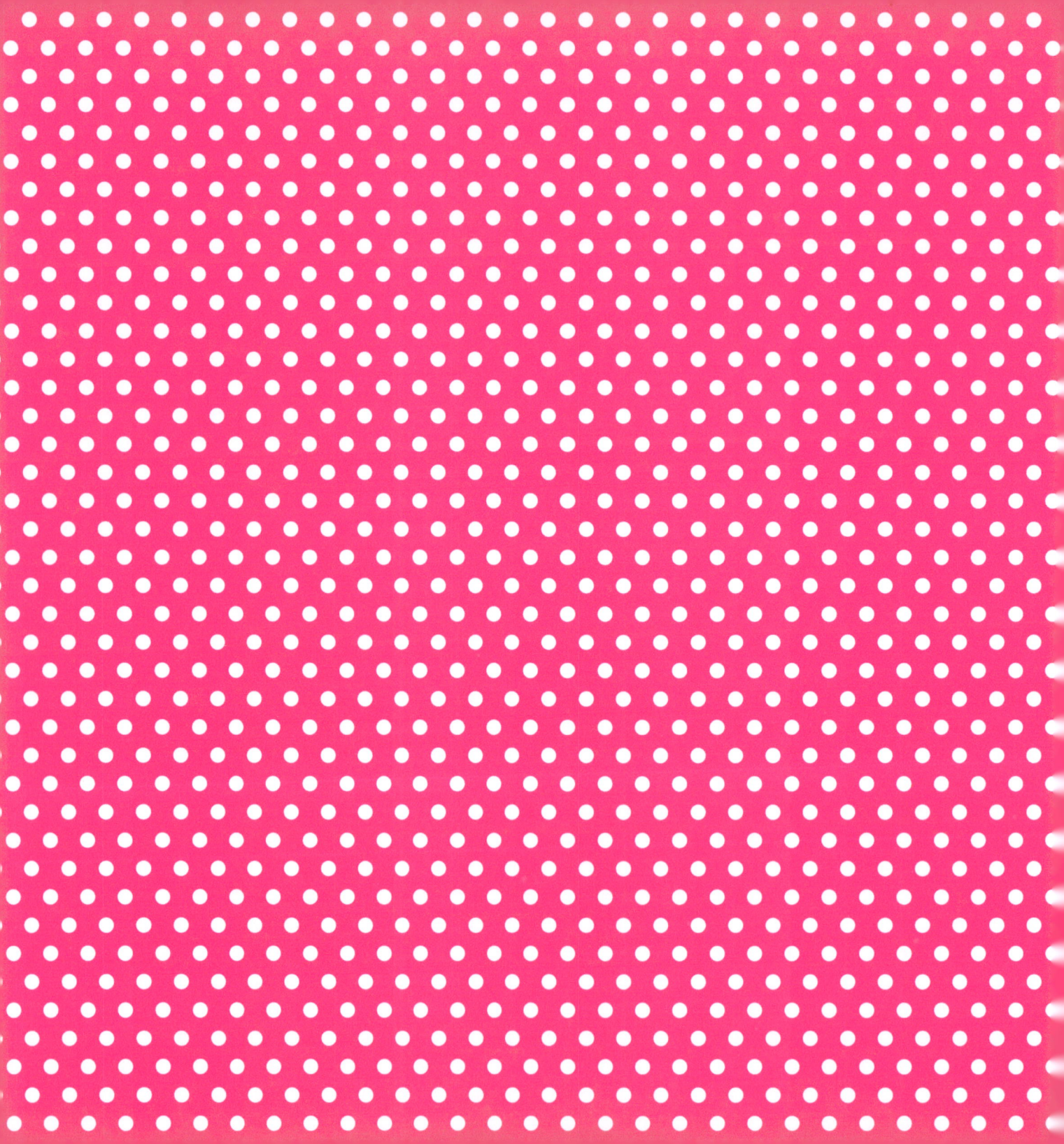

Connect with Your Child Through PLAY...

Find all of our Resources

Books, Videos, Printables, & more at

www.tinytinkles.com

29

Best Friends

30

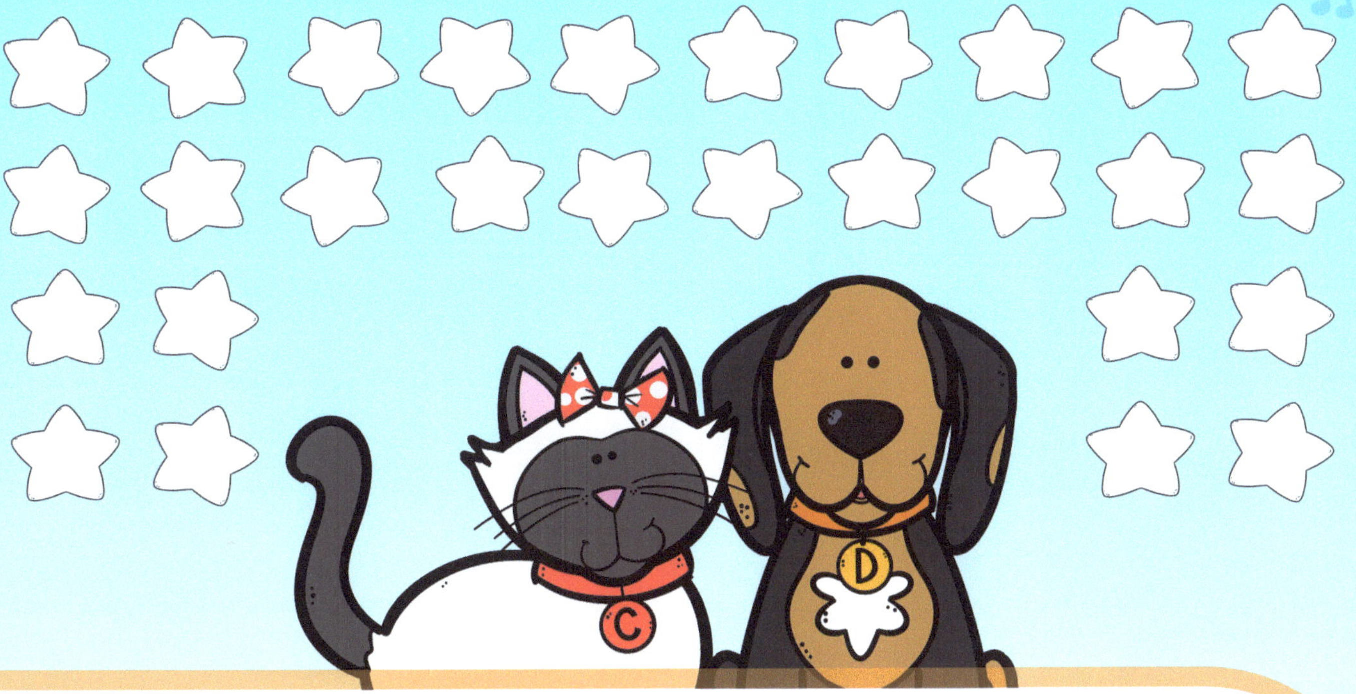
C
D

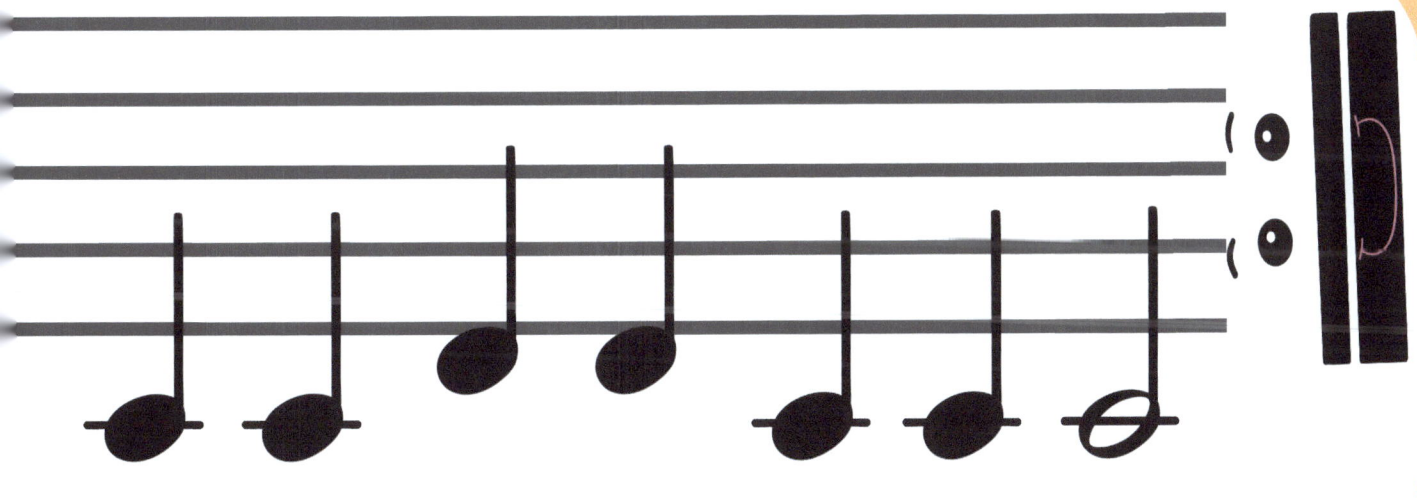

Meow meow woof woof my best friends.

Spooky Boo!

count
1 2 3 4

Spoo   ky   ghost.   Spoo   ky   ghost.

32

End with a **forte** BOO!

Tip   toe   snea   ky   spoo   ky   BOO!

34

End with a big MEOW!

Meow   meow   Chlo   e   Cat.

Meeoow

35

Octopus

End with a big SPLASH!

Splish splash splish splash Oc to pus.

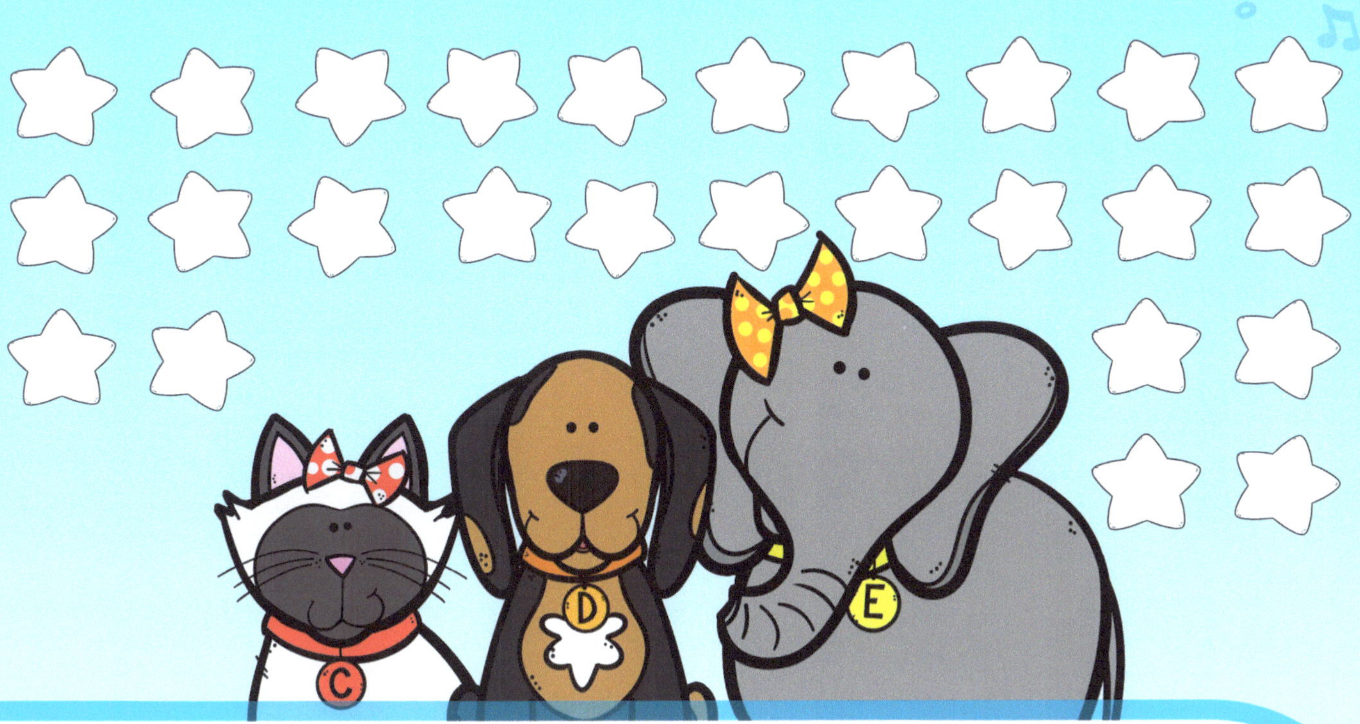
C
D
E

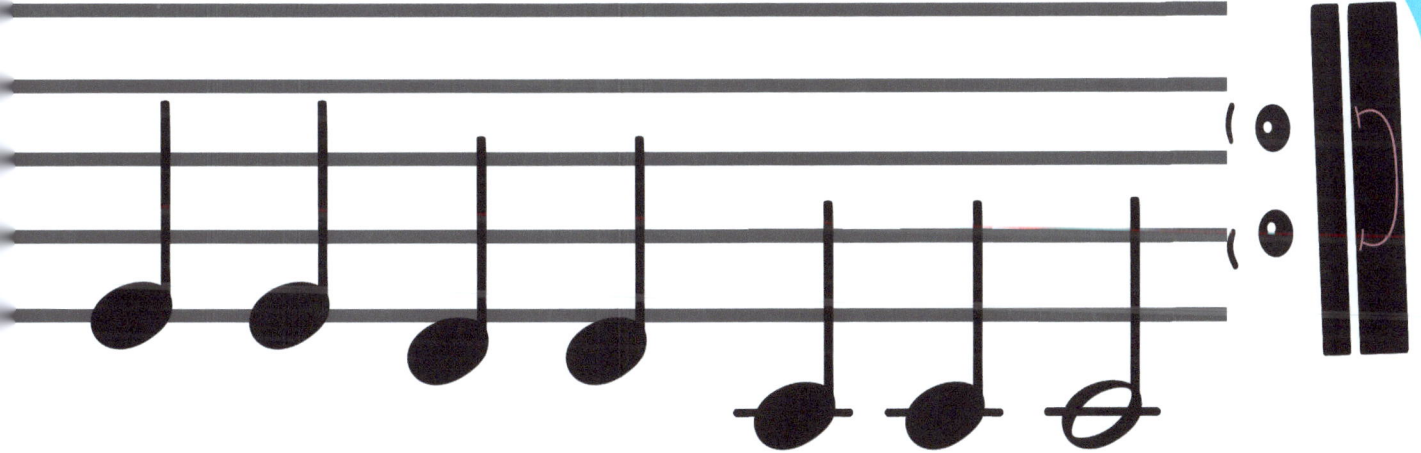

Pah woo woof woof meow meow meow.

40

End with a big WOOF!

Woof woof Dai sy Dog! WOOF!

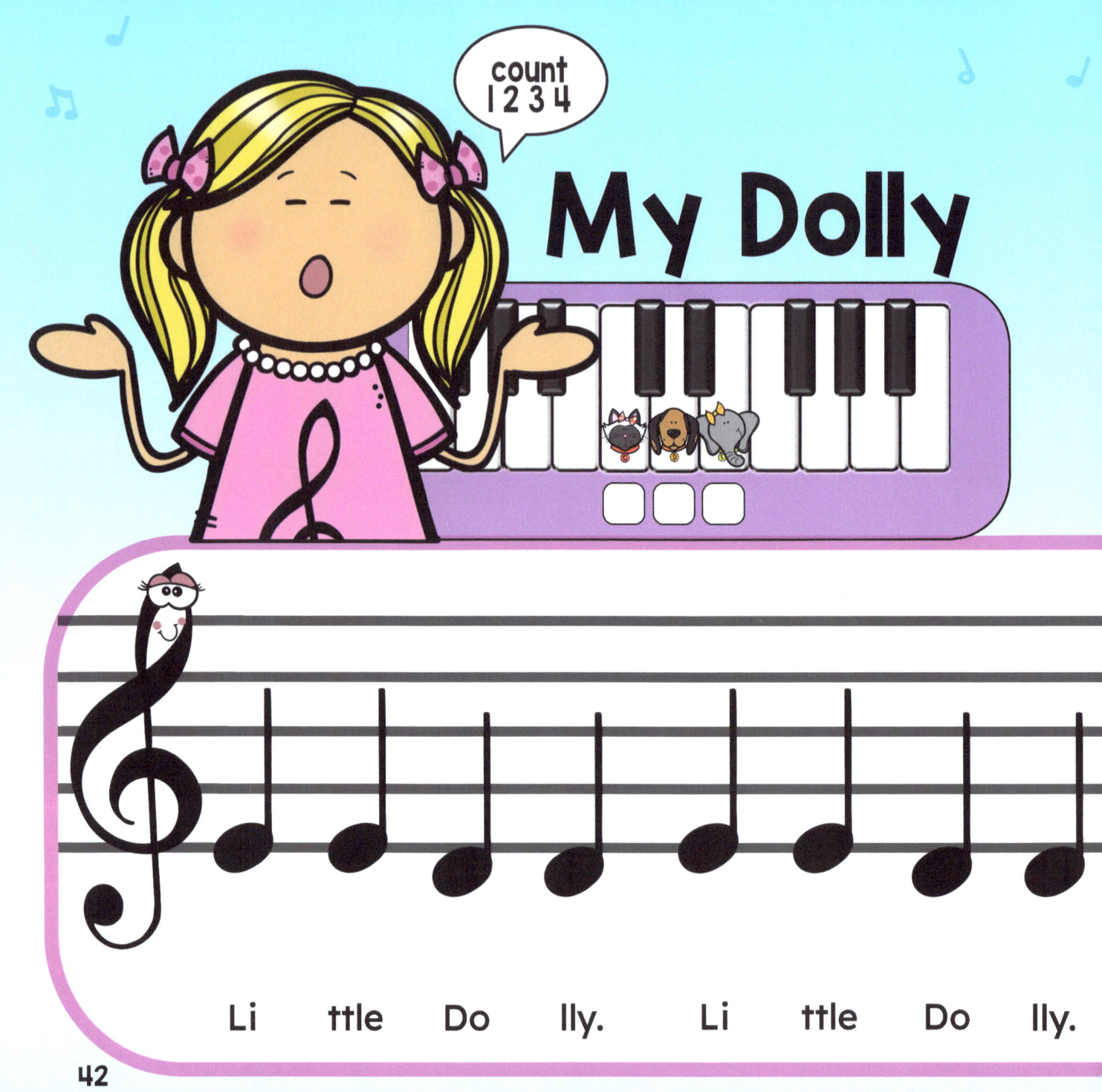

I   love   you!

Apple Pie

count 1 2 3 4

Roll   the   crust,   fill   it   up,

44

45

46

Sweet Jam

count 1 2 3 4

I   love   jam.   Yum   yum   yum!

mmm!

I love sweet straw ber ry jam.

50

she   will   make   us   tea.

Kah! Kah!

52

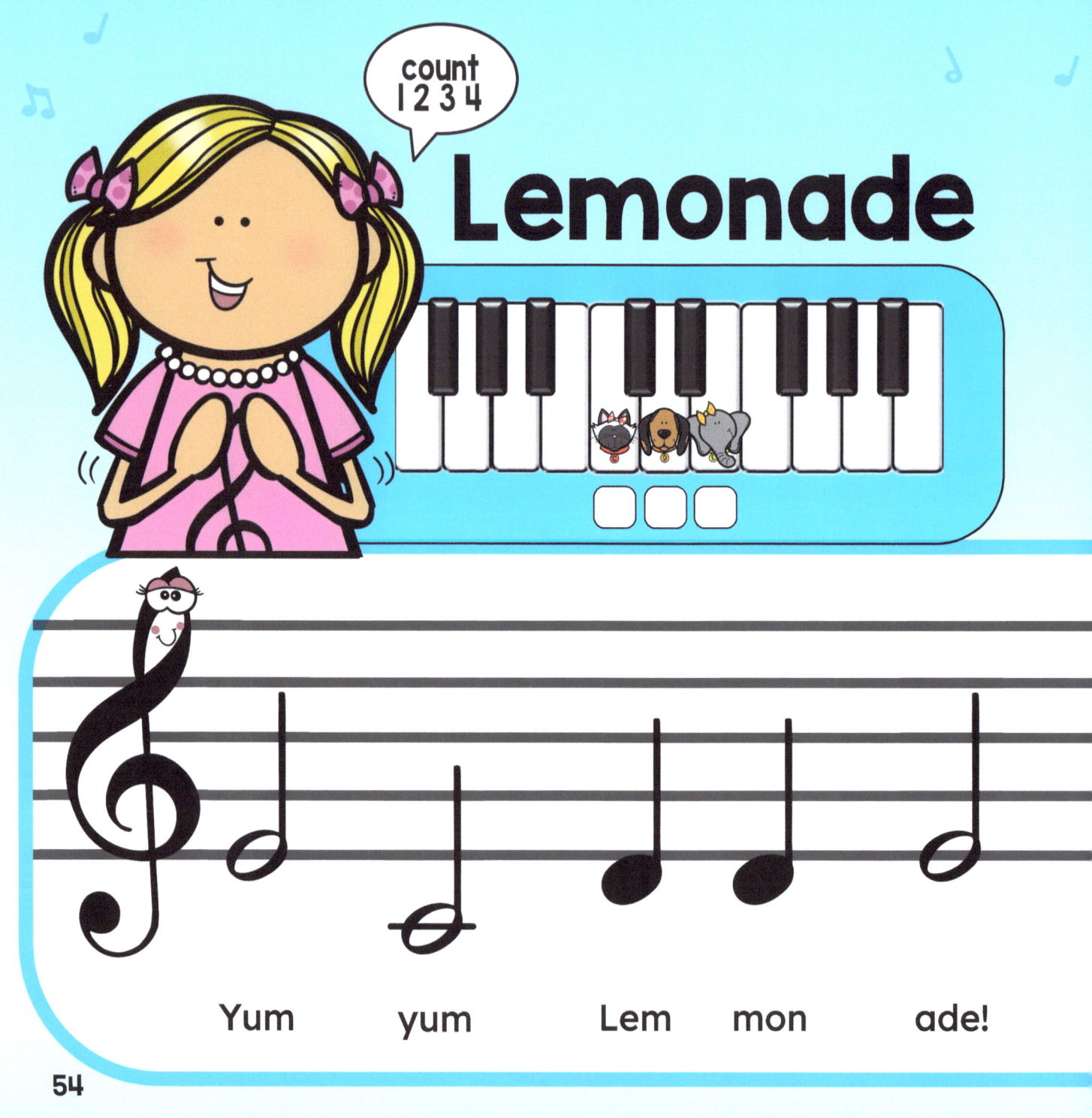

54

End with a big YUM!

Yum yum Lem on ade!

Slurp!

Wiggly Worm

56

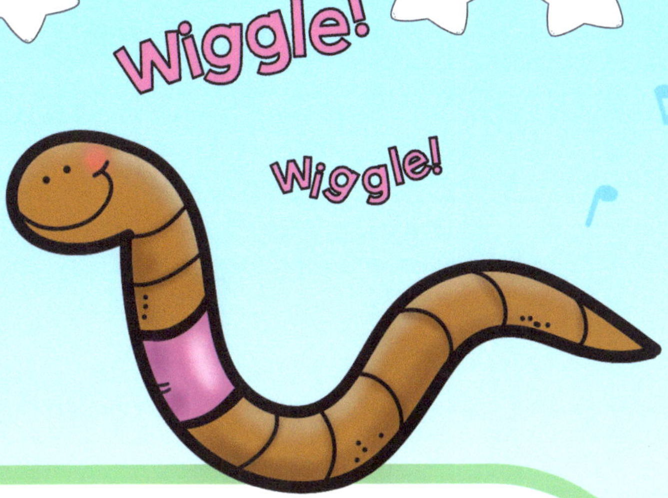
Wiggle!
Wiggle!

Wigg le wigg le wigg ly worm.

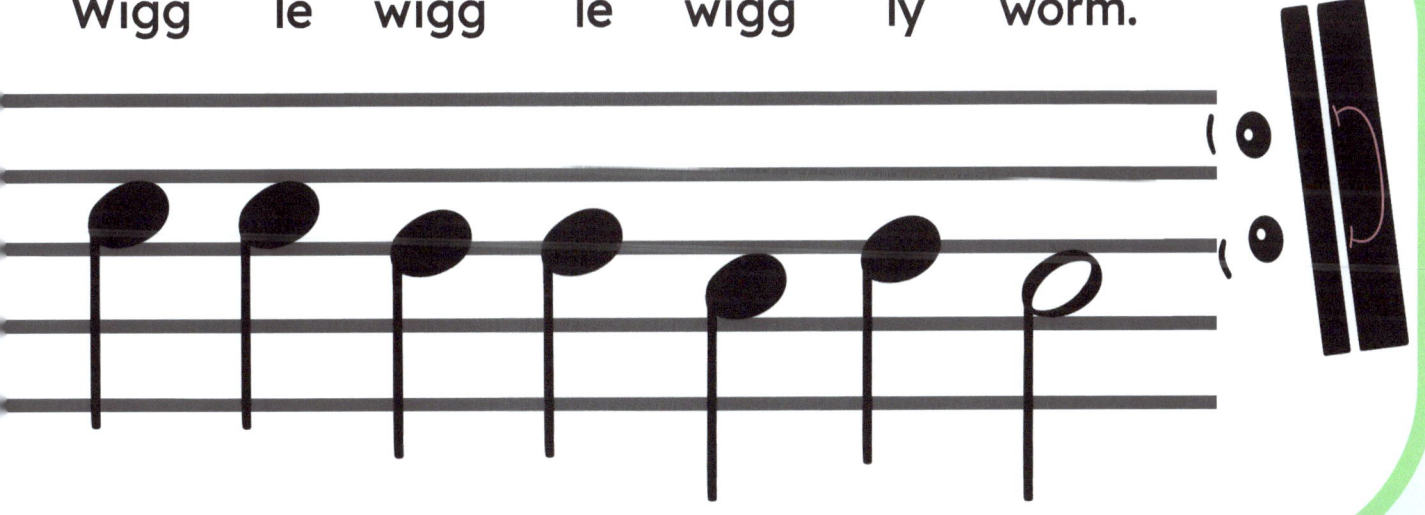

Love our Books?

We LOVE reading your reviews
and hearing your stories!
Please visit us and say

"HELLO"

www.tinytinkles.com

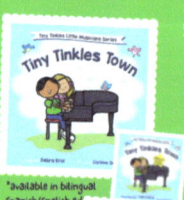

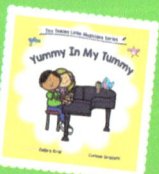

*available in bilingual
Spanish/English Ed.

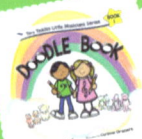

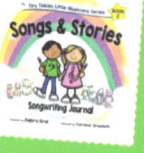

CONGRATULATIONS!

_____

Student's Name

has completed Little Performers Level 5 in the Tiny Tinkles Little Musician Series.

LEVEL 5

_____

Teacher

_____

Date

www.ingramcontent.com/pod-product-compliance
Lightning Source LLC
Chambersburg PA
CBHW041553120626
46551CB00002B/188